JIVE
Goes for a
WALK

....

Ideas and Illustrations by Jamie Graham

Written in Collaboration with
Bridgette Taucher and Erin Boren

Order this book online at www.trafford.com
or email orders@trafford.com

Most Trafford titles are also available at major online book retailers.

 www.trafford.com

North America & international
toll-free: 1 888 232 4444 (USA & Canada)
fax: 812 355 4082

Our mission is to efficiently provide the world's finest, most comprehensive book publishing service, enabling every author to experience success. To find out how to publish your book, your way, and have it available worldwide, visit us online at www.trafford.com

Because of the dynamic nature of the Internet, any web addresses or links contained in this book may have changed since publication and may no longer be valid. The views expressed in this work are solely those of the author and do not necessarily reflect the views of the publisher, and the publisher hereby disclaims any responsibility for them.

ISBN: 978-1-4907-9715-1 (sc)
       978-1-4907-9716-8 (e)

Library of Congress Control Number: 2019914150

Print information available on the last page.

Trafford rev. 09/16/2019

Dedications

This book is for Kirksville Primary School. Thank you for making everything bright and merry for everyone. Remember to **Be a Buddy, Not a Bully.**
Jamie

This book is for my sister Donna, my bother Jeffery, and my niece Lauren. Thank you for making the world so nice for people like me.
Jamie

To Bridgette and Erin, who took my book to heart enough to make it!
With love,
Jamie

Foreword

Jamie's passion for helping and inspiring others is what fuels his writing. Anyone who knows Jamie knows what it means to be truly cared for and treated with kindness. I have been lucky enough to assist Jamie with publishing this book, and I truly believe that anyone who reads it will learn something about themselves and others. Jamie's message is important for people of all ages and his attitude about life is something that everyone should strive to obtain.

Morgan Kemp

Acknowledgements

Thank you Thousand Hills Rotary Club for believing in my cause and helping me move my dream forward.

Love, Jamie

One day, a boy named Jive decided to go for a walk outside his apartment. He was wearing his new high top shoes and he thought he was so cool.

Right outside his door sat Dillon, beeping his horn. Jive said, "Hey kid, beat it. You're so annoying with your nonstop horn beeping! Get out of my way!"

Jive angrily kept walking. Soon, he passed by Alfred who uses a cane so that he won't run into anything. Alfred's cane was close to hitting Jive's shoes. Jive jumped out of the way and screamed, "Hey! Get your stick away from me! Get out of my way!"

Jive was getting more and more angry. He stomped along the sidewalk. When he walked by Amanda, he scuffed his shoe on her wheel. Jive was furious. "You ran over my shoe!" he said, "Stop hogging the whole sidewalk!"

Jive stormed off after yelling at all three people. He couldn't believe that they were all in his way. Suddenly, a chunk of the sky came down and grabbed his shirt. The Sky said, "Jive you're a bully! I can't float up here and watch you be this mean to people!"

"**Y**ou think you're hot stuff, with your big head and fancy shoes, but you're putting a bag over everyone's head by being so mean and inconsiderate!" the Sky continued.

If you looked past people's differences, you would see that everyone has amazing talents. Dillon is fantastic at basketball. You could have a lot of fun playing with him if you got to know him!"

"**A**manda will be your biggest fan if you let her. She is super nice and a great cheerleader."

"**A**lfred is a rockin' dancer, he has rhythm and a fun, goofy personality!"

The Sky was enraged. He told Jive, "If you keep acting like this, you're going to turn into the monster that destroys everyone's happiness!"

After that, the Sky floated back up and Jive walked away feeling very ashamed. He was being a bully. He had no reason to be mean to people just because they were different than him. He decided to apologize.

Jive went to find Dillon and said, "Dillon, I am so sorry for being mean to you, it was really inconsiderate of me. I would love to play basketball with you sometime!"

Dillon smiled and responded, "Thank you for saying sorry. I would love to play basketball with you too!"

After saying sorry to Dillon, Jive went to find Alfred. When Jive found Alfred he said, "Hey Alfred, it's me, Jive. I am so sorry for being mean to you. I should not have yelled at you about your cane. You weren't close to hitting me, I was just being dramatic. I heard you're a great dancer. I'd love to see your dance moves sometime." Alfred forgave him and Jive went to find Amanda.

When Jive found Amanda, he said, "Hi Amanda, earlier I wasn't paying attention, and I scuffed my shoe on your wheel. I am sorry for blaming you. I should watch out and be more courteous to you. Will you forgive me?"

Amanda smiled and said, "I forgive you. I hear you and Dillon are playing basketball sometime. I would love to cheer you guys on!"

Jive grinned and said, "I would love that!"

As Jive hung out with his new friends, he silently looked up and thanked the Sky. Today he learned a very important lesson:

Be a buddy, not a bully.

Printed in the United States
By Bookmasters